WORKBOOK

For

Built from Broken

A Science-Based Guide to Healing
Painful Joints, Preventing Injuries, and
Rebuilding Your Body

A Guide to the book by Scott H. Hogan

Lynne Press

Disclaimer Note

The content provided in this workbook is for informational purposes only. The techniques and strategies discussed are based on personal experiences and should not replace the original book.

Table of Contents

Introduction

Scott H. Hogan conducts an in-depth exploration of overcoming joint discomfort, preventing injuries, and revitalizing your body in this extensive guide. With clarity and expertise, Hogan navigates the intricate terrain of physical rehabilitation, grounded in scientific principles. Whether you're recovering from an injury or seeking proactive joint health strategies, this guide offers tangible insights and practical exercises. "Built from Broken" transcends conventional approaches, presenting a holistic perspective that blends scientific research with real-world applications. Embark on a journey of resilience, understanding, and empowerment as you uncover the secrets to restoring your body's vitality. Through engaging exercises and Hogan's expert guidance, discover the transformative potential inherent in every setback, emerging not merely healed but genuinely built from the broken.

How to Use this Workbook

Embark on an enriching learning experience with this interactive workbook. Utilize the following sections to maximize your understanding and personal growth:

1. **Synopsis:** Commence by reviewing the concise summaries. These encapsulate essential concepts, ensuring a firm foundation for your comprehension.

2. **Essential Takeaways:** Upon completing the chapter, delve deeper into the key takeaways. Ponder how these insights connect to your own communication experiences and challenges.

3. **Self-Reflection Questions:** Engage in introspective exercises using focused

questions. Utilize these prompts to enhance your understanding, fostering personal insights and self-discovery.

4. **Goal Setting:** Establish and define clear goals for yourself. Setting objectives provides direction and purpose,aligning your efforts with meaningful aspirations.

5. **Action Plan:** Translate your goals into practical steps. Craft a realistic plan outlining how you intend to achieve your objectives. This section serves as a roadmap, guiding you along your path to success.

Book Overview

Scott H. Hogan's "Built from Broken" is an insightful guide that combines scientific knowledge with practical advice to help you navigate the intricate process of healing, injury prevention, and physical restoration. Delving into the intricate workings of joints, Hogan unveils the science behind pain and provides a roadmap for recovery. The author meticulously equips readers with concrete techniques to mend aching joints, empowering them to address physical setbacks effectively.

Extending beyond rehabilitation, the book presents a proactive approach to injury prevention. Hogan emphasizes the significance of understanding one's body, enabling readers to make informed decisions for long-term well-being. The narrative seamlessly interweaves Hogan's personal experiences, anecdotes, and engaging case studies, crafting a compelling story that resonates with both fitness novices and enthusiasts.

"Built from Broken" transcends a mere how-to manual; it stands as a testament to resilience and the human body's remarkable ability to heal. Whether grappling with chronic pain, seeking to prevent injuries, or pursuing a holistic approach to rebuilding your physical self, Hogan's authoritative voice and evidence-based recommendations make this book an indispensable resource on your journey toward achieving physical well-being.

Chapter 1: A Case for Load Training

Scott H. Hogan lays the foundation for the book's central theme: the transformative power of load training in alleviating joint pain, preventing injuries, and rebuilding the body. He begins by highlighting the widespread prevalence of musculoskeletal disorders and joint discomfort, underscoring the need for effective solutions that go beyond conventional approaches. Delving into the science of load training, he presents compelling evidence that it promotes joint health and overall well-being.

Hogan further explores the concept of load training, emphasizing its role in strengthening not only muscles but also the connective tissues crucial for joint stability. Drawing upon scientific evidence, he makes a persuasive case for load training as both a preventive measure against injuries and a rehabilitative therapy for individuals currently experiencing joint discomfort. The chapter serves as a comprehensive guide, addressing common load training misconceptions and revealing its intricate benefits.

Readers are equipped with practical insights, actionable recommendations, and a roadmap for incorporating load training into their exercise routines. Hogan emphasizes the importance of personalized strategies that consider individual fitness levels and specific joint concerns. By weaving together real-world examples, scientific data, and his own expertise,Chapter 1 provides an engaging introduction to the fundamental principle underpinning "Built from Broken." It not only advocates for the transformative potential of load training but also instills in readers a sense of empowerment,encouraging them to embrace this science-backed practice for enhanced joint health and physical resilience.

Key Points

- Prioritize load training for improved joint health.
- Grasp the scientific underpinnings of load training's effectiveness.

- Personalize your approach based on your fitness level and joint concerns.

Self-Reflection Questions

- How can I integrate load training into my current workout routine?

_____

_____

_____

_____

_____

_____

_____

- What load training myths do I need to debunk?

- What specific joint issues or concerns should I address in my fitness journey?

_____

_____

_____

_____

Goals

- Incorporate regular load training
  sessions to enhance joint strength.
- Challenge and modify preconceived
  notions about fitness and joint health.
- Customize exercise programs to cater
  to the unique needs of each joint.

Action Plan

1. Research and select suitable load
   training exercises.

2. Utilize educational resources to gain a deeper understanding of load training's benefits.
3. Collaborate with a fitness professional to develop a personalized load training plan aligned with your joint health goals.

Chapter 2: The Anatomy of Pain

Scott H. Hogan embarks on an insightful exploration of the perplexing realm of pain, delving into the underlying anatomy that contributes to its enigmatic nature. Hogan commences by dissecting the physiological foundations of pain, shedding light on the intricate interplay between neurons, muscles, and joints. He meticulously unravels the neurological pathways,explaining how the brain receives and interprets signals of distress. Hogan masterfully investigates the role of neurotransmitters and their influence on pain perception, empowering readers with a sophisticated understanding of the molecular mechanisms at play.

The author then ventures into the domain of chronic pain, unveiling the mechanisms that transform acute discomfort into enduring suffering. Hogan skillfully demonstrates how chronic pain can rewire the neural system, giving rise to a self-perpetuating cycle that intensifies distress. He seamlessly integrates real-world examples and case studies throughout the chapter, humanizing scientific terminology and rendering it accessible to a wide range of readers.

Hogan also sheds light on the psychological dimensions of pain, illuminating the intricate connections between mind and body. He explores the impact of stress, emotions, and mental health on pain perception and treatment, emphasizing the necessity of a holistic approach to rehabilitation. By meticulously unraveling the anatomy of pain, Hogan empowers readers with the knowledge necessary to make informed decisions about their health.

Chapter 2 serves as a foundational exploration of the intricate anatomy of pain, equipping readers with the tools to comprehend the complexities of their own bodily sensations. Hogan's masterful blend of scientific rigor and compassionate storytelling transforms this chapter into an essential read for anyone seeking to navigate the challenging landscape of physical discomfort and embark on a journey toward healing and resilience.

Key Points

- Pain arises from a intricate interplay of neurological, physiological, and psychological factors.
- Chronic pain is distinguished by a self-perpetuating cycle that rewires the neural system.
- Effective pain management necessitates a comprehensive approach that addresses both the physical and emotional aspects of pain.

Self-Reflection Questions

1. How does my perception of pain impact my coping strategies?

_____

_____

_____

_____

_____

_____

_____

_____

2. How do stress and emotions influence my pain experience?

_____

_____

_____

_____

_____

_____

_____

_____

_____

_____

3. Am I adopting a holistic approach to pain management?

_____

_____

_____

_____

_____

_____

_____

_____

_____

Goals

1. Acquire a comprehensive understanding of the physiological and psychological dimensions of my suffering.
2. Formulate strategies to break the cycle of chronic pain through informed decisions.
3. Prioritize a holistic approach to well-being, encompassing both physical and emotional aspects.

Action Plan

1. Delve into credible sources to learn about the anatomy of pain.
2. Integrate stress-reducing activities into my daily routine.
3. Collaborate with healthcare professionals to develop a tailored,

comprehensive pain management
plan.

Chapter 3: What to Focus on Instead of Pain Relief

This chapter unveils a transformative approach to repairing damaged joints and restoring the body. Hogan guides readers away from the conventional focus on pain relief, advocating for a shift toward holistic solutions for long-term well-being. The chapter emphasizes the importance of understanding the root causes of joint pain rather than merely addressing symptoms. Hogan introduces readers to scientific concepts that empower them to focus on strengthening and training their bodies to address the underlying issues that contribute to pain.

The chapter's primary focus lies in proactive measures that extend beyond seeking immediate alleviation. Hogan delves into the significance of specific activities, diet, and lifestyle factors in promoting joint health. Readers are encouraged to adopt a holistic perspective, viewing pain as a signal rather than an obstacle. The chapter advocates for the development of resilience through targeted exercises that enhance joint mobility, stability, and strength. Hogan underscores the importance of proper nutrition in supporting the body's natural healing processes, emphasizing the impact of a balanced diet on joint health.

The author introduces mindfulness practices and stress management strategies as crucial components of the healing process. By shifting the emphasis from urgent pain treatment to long-term well-being, readers gain a proactive toolkit for joint health and injury prevention. Hogan's evidence-based approach guides readers through their unique healing journeys,fostering a mindset shift toward long-term rehabilitation. Chapter 3 serves as an essential guide, steering readers away from the reactive pursuit of pain alleviation and towards a proactive, science-backed strategy to repair and fortify the body against future challenges.

Key Points

1. Shift the focus from immediate pain relief to identifying and addressing underlying causes for long-term joint health.

2. Embrace a holistic approach that encompasses exercise, nutrition, and mindfulness practices.
3. Recognize pain as an indicator of potential problems and foster resilience through proactive measures.

Self-Reflection Questions

1. What are the root causes of my joint pain, and how can I actively address them?

_____

_____

_____

_____

_____

2. Do I incorporate specific activities, a
    healthy diet, and stress management
    techniques into my daily routine?

_____

_____

_____

_____

3. How can I reframe my perception of
   pain, transforming it from an obstacle
   to a driving force for positive change?

_____

_____

_____

_____

_____

_____

_____

Goals

1. Prioritize a comprehensive approach
   to joint health by integrating targeted
   exercises, a balanced diet, and
   mindfulness practices into daily
   routines.

2. Cultivate resilience by acknowledging pain as a warning signal and taking preventive steps.
3. Encourage a shift in perspective from instant relief to long-term well-being.

Action Plan

1. Develop a personalized workout plan that emphasizes joint mobility, stability, and strength.
2. Adopt a balanced and nutritious diet to support the body's natural healing processes.
3. Integrate mindfulness practices and stress management techniques into daily life for holistic well-being.

Chapter 4: How to Train Your Collagen

The author explores the crucial subject of optimizing collagen training for enhanced joint health and overall bodily resilience. The chapter commences by elucidating the pivotal role of collagen in sustaining joints, tendons, and ligaments, underscoring its significance in maintaining overall structural integrity. Hogan adeptly merges scientific insights with actionable advice, furnishing readers with a comprehensive understanding of the versatile nature of collagen.

Within the chapter, various exercise techniques tailored specifically to enhance collagen strength and flexibility are thoroughly examined. Hogan presents a range of workouts and routines crafted to stimulate collagen formation, emphasizing the importance of progressive loading for promoting tissue adaptability. He guides readers through the incorporation of these exercises into their fitness regimens, ensuring a well-rounded and targeted approach to collagen training.

A notable highlight of this chapter is Hogan's emphasis on personalized training strategies. Acknowledging the diverse demands and circumstances of individuals, he provides adaptable guidelines, empowering readers to tailor their collagen training to suit their unique needs. Readers gain practical insights to customize their training programs, whether for recovering from an injury or proactively preventing joint issues.

Hogan also delves into the significance of nutrition in collagen health, elucidating how dietary choices impact the body's ability to repair and construct connective tissues. He demystifies the correlation between nutrition and collagen production, bridging scientific principles with actionable suggestions, enabling readers to make informed decisions that support their journey of healing and reconstruction.

Chapter 4 serves as a comprehensive guide on "How to Train Your Collagen," seamlessly integrating scientific knowledge with practical applications. Hogan's approach empowers readers to take charge of their joint health, providing a roadmap not only for alleviating pain and averting injuries but also for rejuvenating and fortifying their bodies for enduring well-being.

Key Points

1. Maintaining collagen flexibility is essential for joint health.
2. Customized training promotes collagen strength and resilience.
3. Proper nutrition plays a crucial role in collagen production.

Self-Reflection Questions

1. How can I modify exercises to suit my specific needs and limitations?

2. What dietary choices can support my collagen health and joint function?

3. Am I gradually increasing the load on my movements for optimal collagen adaptation?

_____

_____

_____

_____

_____

_____

_____

_____

Goals

1. Enhance collagen strength to improve joint durability and prevent injuries.
2. Design personalized training regimens that align with individual needs and preferences.
3. Make informed food choices to promote collagen synthesis and overall well-being.

Action Plan

1. Incorporate progressive loading exercises into your workout routine to stimulate collagen production.
2. Personalize exercises based on your injury history, fitness level, and specific goals.

3. Consult with a healthcare professional or nutritionist for personalized guidance on collagen-boosting foods and supplements.

Chapter 5: Movement: The Original Mobility

Scott H. Hogan delves into the fundamental concept of movement as the foundation of mobility. He explores the intricate interplay between movement and our bodies' inherent capacity to maintain mobility. Hogan emphasizes an evolutionary perspective, asserting that our ancestors' survival was inextricably linked to their ability to move in diverse ways. The chapter elucidates how modern sedentary lifestyles have disrupted this natural connection to mobility, leading to a plethora of joint problems and injuries.

Hogan introduces readers to the notion of "primal mobility," highlighting the vast range of movements that our bodies are designed to perform. Our joints and muscles are inherently equipped to execute a wide spectrum of activities, from walking and running to more complex movements. The author underscores the significance of preserving these natural motions for overall joint health and injury prevention, supported by scientific evidence.

The chapter provides practical guidance on incorporating unique mobility exercises into daily routines. Hogan outlines a systematic approach to progressively reintroduce movement diversity, empowering readers to reclaim their bodies' innate mobility. By interweaving scientific data and practical advice, the chapter aims to motivate readers to break free from the constraints of a sedentary lifestyle and cultivate a more active and resilient physique.

This chapter stands as a pivotal element in Hogan's book, illuminating the critical importance of diverse and natural movements in healing injured joints, preventing injuries, and rebuilding the body. It invites readers to embrace the evolutionary wisdom embedded within our bodies, advocating for a return to the fundamental principle that movement is an essential component in the intricate dance of joint health and physical resilience.

Key Points

1. Embrace the evolutionary wisdom that emphasizes diverse movements for joint health.
2. Counteract the effects of a sedentary lifestyle by incorporating novel mobility exercises.
3. Prioritize dynamic activities to prevent injuries and promote physical restoration.

Self-Reflection Questions

1. Does my daily routine encompass a variety of movements?

2. How has a sedentary lifestyle
impacted my joint health?

3. What unique mobility exercises can I integrate to enhance my physical resilience?

_____

_____

_____

_____

_____

_____

_____

Goals

1. Expand the range of movements in my daily routine.
2. Minimize sedentary behavior.

3. Enhance joint health through targeted activities.

Action Plan

1. Schedule brief mobility sessions throughout the day.
2. Identify and modify sedentary habits.
3. Implement a weekly routine of unique mobility exercises to promote overall joint health.

Chapter 6:
Science-Backed Mobility Training

This chapter delves into the realm of scientifically supported mobility training, offering readers a comprehensive manual for enhancing joint health, mitigating injuries, and rejuvenating the body. Hogan systematically dissects the intricacies of mobility training, relying on scientific principles to illustrate its efficacy. The chapter initiates by exploring the physiological foundations of mobility, scrutinizing how specific exercises can enhance joint function and flexibility. Hogan adeptly integrates research findings to underscore the importance of incorporating evidence-based approaches into one's exercise regimen.

Going beyond conventional methods, the author explores the biomechanics of distinct exercises and their impact on joint health. Readers gain insights into the intricate interplay between muscle activation, range of motion, and injury prevention. Hogan substantiates his observations with research demonstrating a correlation between structured mobility exercises and a reduction in cases of joint pain and damage.

The practical application of scientific information stands out as a primary feature of this chapter. Hogan provides readers with a diverse array of mobility exercises, each supported by scientific evidence. From dynamic stretches to targeted joint exercises, the author instructs readers on customizing their mobility routines according to individual needs and objectives. The chapter underscores the importance of progression, guiding readers through a gradual process to enhance mobility over time.

Chapter 6 serves as a guiding beacon for those seeking a robust, evidence-based approach to enhance joint health and prevent injuries. Hogan's comprehensive integration of scientific knowledge, coupled with practical guidance, elevates this chapter to essential reading for anyone on a journey to rebuild their body and overcome physical limitations.

Key Points

1. Prioritize research-backed mobility exercises for enhanced joint health.
2. Grasp the biomechanics of movement to minimize injury risk.
3. Employ gradual progression for long-term mobility improvement.

Self-Reflection Questions

1. Do I incorporate scientifically validated mobility exercises into my routine?

2. Am I aware of potential injury
   triggers and do I understand the
   biomechanics of my movements?

3. Is my mobility training progressing steadily and effectively?

_____

_____

_____

_____

_____

_____

_____

_____

Goals

1. Enhance joint flexibility and function.

2. Reduce the likelihood of injuries by performing targeted mobility exercises.
3. Develop a systematic, gradual mobility regimen.

Action Plan

1. Research and implement evidence-based mobility exercises.
2. Comprehend the biomechanics of essential movements to improve injury prevention.
3. Create a personalized, step-by-step progression plan for ongoing mobility development.

Chapter 7: Corrective Routines

The chapter elucidates the pivotal role of corrective routines in the journey to alleviate joint discomfort, prevent injuries, and reconstruct the body. Hogan underscores the significance of targeted exercises crafted to rectify specific musculoskeletal imbalances and deficiencies. Commencing with an exploration of the science behind corrective routines, the chapter highlights their crucial role in reinstating healthy movement patterns and functionality to compromised joints. Hogan adeptly guides readers through an array of exercises, encompassing mobility drills and strength-building regimens, all designed to address postural distortions and biomechanical irregularities.

This comprehensive guide enlightens readers on the intricacies of body mechanics, enabling them to identify areas of weakness or imbalance that could contribute to joint discomfort or injury. Hogan adopts a systematic approach, empowering individuals to formulate a customized remedial practice tailored to their unique needs. Rather than offering a generic set of exercises, the chapter equips readers with the knowledge to assess their own bodies and construct a personalized progression strategy. Hogan underscores the importance of consistency and gradual improvement in these routines, emphasizing the need for patience to achieve lasting results.

Real-world examples and case studies are interwoven to illustrate how individuals have effectively employed corrective routines to overcome physical challenges. By demystifying the science underpinning corrective workouts and providing practical guidance, Hogan encourages readers to take charge of their physical well-being. Essentially, Chapter 7 acts as a guide for readers to navigate the intricate terrain of corrective routines, fostering a heightened awareness of their bodies and facilitating the journey toward optimal joint health and overall physical resilience.

Key Points

1. Identifying specific musculoskeletal imbalances is crucial for designing effective corrective exercises.

2. Consistency is the key to achieving long-lasting results from corrective exercise programs.

3. Understanding the science behind corrective exercises empowers individuals to make informed decisions about their physical well-being.

Self-Reflection Questions

1. Have you identified any areas of weakness or imbalance in your body?

_____

_____

_____

_____

_____

_____

_____

_____

2. How can you incorporate corrective
   exercises into your daily or weekly
   routine?

_____

_____

_____

_____

_____

_____

_____

_____

_____

3. Are you prepared to commit to the gradual progression required for long-term improvement?

_____

_____

_____

_____

_____

_____

_____

_____

_____

Goals

1. Develop a personalized corrective exercise program to address specific musculoskeletal imbalances.
2. Maintain consistent engagement in corrective exercises, either daily or weekly.
3. Enhance your understanding of body mechanics and the role of corrective practices in promoting joint health.

Action Plan

1. Conduct a self-assessment or seek professional guidance to identify areas that require corrective attention.
2. Schedule dedicated time for corrective exercises in your daily or weekly routine.
3. Educate yourself on the scientific principles underlying corrective

exercises to maximize their effectiveness.

Chapter 8: Preventing the Big Three

The chapter unveils crucial strategies for averting three common hurdles in joint health and physical resilience. Hogan leverages scientific expertise to guide readers in navigating challenges that often hinder individuals on their journey to physical well-being. The "Big Three" encompass significant challenges like joint discomfort, injuries, and the overall process of bodily regeneration. Hogan meticulously explores preventive measures, melding biomechanical principles with practical advice to empower readers with the knowledge to safeguard their joints and bodies from these prevalent issues.

Throughout the chapter, Hogan underscores the importance of comprehending the root causes of joint discomfort, injuries, and bodily degeneration. By dissecting the underlying science, readers gain a comprehensive understanding of how to effectively counteract these challenges. The author advocates for a proactive approach involving specific exercises, lifestyle modifications, and nutritional considerations to diminish the likelihood of encountering the "Big Three." Hogan's insights are not only rooted in scientific research but also draw from his practical experience, rendering the advice accessible and applicable to a diverse audience.

The chapter unfolds as a roadmap, guiding readers through a multimodal preventative approach. Hogan presents a holistic framework for readers to embrace and integrate into their daily lives, from refining movement patterns to fostering joint resilience through strength training. By emphasizing the importance of injury prevention and body maintenance, Hogan empowers individuals to take charge of their physical well-being.

Chapter 8 stands as a pivotal guide in "Built from Broken," offering readers a wealth of knowledge and practical solutions to circumvent the challenges of the "Big Three"—joint discomfort, injuries, and the rebuilding process. Hogan's amalgamation of scientific insights and practical advice makes this chapter a valuable resource for anyone aspiring to cultivate a robust and healthy body.

Key Points

1. Prioritize proactive joint care by engaging in targeted exercises and cultivating biomechanical awareness.
2. Grasp the scientific principles underpinning joint health to effectively prevent pain and injuries.
3. Embrace a holistic approach to body resilience, incorporating nutritional modifications and lifestyle changes.

Self-Reflection Questions

1. What actions can I take to enhance my biomechanical understanding and safeguard my joints?

_____

_____

_____

_____

_____

_____

_____

_____

2. What lifestyle adjustments can I make to improve my body's overall resilience?

_____

_____

_____

_____

_____

_____

_____

3. Do I consistently integrate joint health prevention activities into my routine?

Goals

1. Establish a regular exercise program that incorporates joint-strengthening activities.
2. Implement dietary strategies to support the body's overall resilience.
3. Foster a mindset shift towards proactive, rather than reactive, approaches to joint health management.

Action Plan

1. Research and incorporate biomechanically sound exercises into your daily workout routine.
2. Identify and incorporate joint-friendly foods into your regular diet for long-term health.
3. Develop a weekly schedule for preventative exercises and adhere to it diligently.

Chapter 9: Injury Recovery: Strategy and Tactics

Scott initiates by exploring the science behind optimal recovery, underscoring the importance of understanding the body's innate healing mechanisms. He delves into the nuanced principles of joint regeneration, providing readers with crucial insights into the origins of injuries and their impact on the body.

The chapter delves into specific injury recovery techniques, encompassing both the physical and mental dimensions of the healing process. Hogan introduces evidence-based strategies to expedite and enhance recovery. His approach offers a comprehensive plan to rejuvenate the body post-injury, covering specific activities and nutritional recommendations. Recognizing the uniqueness of each person's healing journey, the author emphasizes the necessity of an individualized treatment approach.

Scott sheds light on the psychological aspects of injury recovery, acknowledging the emotional toll injuries may exact. He presents practical methods for maintaining a positive mindset throughout the rehabilitation journey, stressing the interconnectedness of mental and physical well-being. By blending scientific knowledge with practical advice, Hogan provides readers with a guide to navigate the complexities of injury rehabilitation.

This chapter serves as an invaluable guide for anyone facing the challenges of injury recovery. Hogan's evidence-based approach, coupled with strategic insights and practical techniques, equips readers not only to address sore joints but also to prevent future injuries. The chapter's focus on a comprehensive healing strategy, encompassing both physical and emotional aspects, positions it as essential reading for those on the path to restoring their bodies after a setback.

Key Points

1. Delve into the science behind injury recovery.
2. Embrace a holistic approach to healing, encompassing mind, body, and spirit.
3. Personalize your rehabilitation strategy for optimal outcomes.

Self-Reflection Questions

1. To what extent do I comprehend my body's natural healing processes?

_____

_____

_____

_____

_____

2. How can I cultivate a positive mindset
   throughout the recovery journey?

_____

_____

_____

_____

_____

_____

_____

_____

_____

_____

3. Have I tailored my rehabilitation plan
   to address my specific needs and
   limitations?

_____

_____

_____

_____

_____

_____

_____

_____

_____

Goals

1. Gain a comprehensive understanding of injury healing science.
2. Nurture mental well-being through mindfulness practices and stress management techniques.

3. Develop an individualized rehabilitation plan that aligns with personal requirements and progress.

Action Plan

1. Engage in educational resources to understand the scientific principles underlying injury recovery.
2. Incorporate mind-body activities such as meditation and yoga into your daily routine to promote mental well-being.
3. Collaborate with healthcare professionals to design a personalized rehabilitation plan that addresses your specific injury and recovery goals.

Chapter 10: Why it's Smart to be Disciplined

This chapter delves into the crucial aspects of workout programming and periodization, highlighting the intelligence behind maintaining consistency in one's fitness regimen. Through a comprehensive workout routine, the author underscores a science-based approach to alleviating joint discomfort, preventing injuries, and fostering body repair. Hogan advocates for a systematic and disciplined approach to exercise programming, emphasizing the benefits of periodization—a structured method of scheduling training to optimize performance and recovery. The chapter underscores the importance of thoughtful and strategic workout planning, recognizing the dynamic and ever-changing nature of the body's response to exercise.

Hogan elucidates the significance of understanding one's own body, customizing routines to individual needs, and recognizing the value of progression. The chapter explores the science of periodization, elucidating how it maximizes physical gains while minimizing the risk of overtraining and injury. It advocates for a balance of intensity and recovery in one's fitness journey, promoting long-term sustainability. Hogan guides readers through the process of setting realistic goals and adjusting workout plans to individual capacities, cultivating a smart and resilient sense of discipline.

The chapter delves into the psychological aspects of exercise discipline, underscoring the importance of consistency in achieving desired outcomes. Hogan empowers readers to make informed fitness decisions by delving into the rationale behind disciplined workout programs. Overall, Chapter 9 serves as a comprehensive guide, seamlessly blending scientific principles with practical advice to inspire readers to approach exercise with intelligence, discipline, and a focus on long-term success.

Key Points

1. Prioritize structured exercise programming to safeguard joint health and prevent injuries.

2. Implement periodization strategies to optimize performance and achieve long-term fitness goals.
3. Maintain a balanced approach that integrates both training intensity and recovery for long-term well-being.

Self-Reflection Questions

1. Do I currently tailor my workout program to address the specific needs of my body?

_____

_____

_____

_____

_____

2. Is my current training plan sustainable
   in the long term, aligning with my
   long-term fitness aspirations?

3. Do I possess a clear understanding of
   the science behind periodization and
   its implications for my fitness
   journey?

_____

_____

_____

_____

_____

_____

_____

_____

Goals

1. Embark on a structured fitness
   program that prioritizes joint health.

2. Incorporate periodization principles into my workout routine to enhance outcomes.
3. Cultivate a balanced approach that harmonizes training intensity with adequate recovery periods.

Action Plan

1. Conduct thorough research and design a personalized workout regimen that emphasizes joint-friendly exercises.
2. Plan a monthly periodized training schedule that incorporates gradual increases in intensity.
3. Regularly monitor and adjust my training regimen, emphasizing consistency and adequate recovery.

Chapter 11: Mastering the Movement

This chapter delves into the crucial aspect of mastering physical movements to facilitate healing, prevent injuries, and reconstruct the body. Hogan underscores the significance of understanding and mastering a range of movements, from basic patterns to more intricate exercises. The chapter advocates for a scientific approach, leveraging biomechanics and anatomy to assist readers in executing actions with precision and efficiency.

Hogan begins by elucidating the correlation between good mobility and joint health. He explores how learning fundamental movements enhances joint stability and functionality, offering a preventive strategy for common issues. The chapter equips readers with practical insights to identify and rectify movement abnormalities, empowering them to actively participate in their recovery process.

Progressive workouts tailored to individual needs are presented in this chapter, supporting a gradual and sustainable approach to body reconstruction. Hogan underscores the importance of consistency and patience in this process, emphasizing that mastering movement involves neuromuscular control and coordination as much as strength.

The author translates scientific concepts into practical guidance, encouraging readers to apply their newfound knowledge in their daily lives. This allows individuals to seamlessly integrate movement mastery into their everyday routines, enhancing long-term joint health and overall well-being. Hogan's expertise shines through as he guides readers through a comprehensive approach to movement, blending science, pragmatism, and a genuine understanding of the challenges inherent in physical rehabilitation.

Chapter 11 provides readers with a comprehensive strategy for mastering their movements, offering a pathway to healing, injury prevention, and body restoration based on sound scientific principles and practical applications.

Key Points

1. Prioritize fundamental joint-health movements for optimal joint function.
2. Employ a scientific approach to identify and rectify movement imbalances that may contribute to joint pain or dysfunction.
3. Integrate progressive exercises into your daily routine to facilitate long-term body restoration and enhance physical resilience.

Self-Reflection Questions

1. Do your daily activities promote joint health and movement diversity?

_____

_____

_____

_____

_____

_____

_____

_____

_____

2. Have you identified and addressed
   any existing movement imbalances

that could be affecting your joint
health?

_____

_____

_____

_____

_____

_____

_____

_____

_____

3. Do you regularly incorporate progressive exercises into your routine to gradually improve your movement capabilities and overall physical well-being?

_____

_____

_____

_____

_____

_____

_____

_____

Goals

1. Enhance joint stability and range of motion by mastering fundamental movements.
2. Utilize targeted exercises to correct identified movement abnormalities and restore optimal body alignment.
3. Integrate progressive exercises into daily routines to promote holistic body regeneration and enhance physical resilience.

Action Plan

1. Dedicate time each day to practice fundamental joint-health movements, ensuring proper form and technique.

2. Consult with a healthcare professional or movement specialist to assess your movement patterns and identify any potential imbalances or dysfunctions that may require corrective exercises.

3. Develop a progressive exercise plan that gradually increases the intensity, duration, and complexity of your workouts to challenge your body and promote long-term physical improvement.

Chapter 12: The BFB Training Program

Hogan delves into the fundamental concepts of the BFB Training Program, offering readers a structured pathway to enhance their physical well-being. The program integrates therapeutic exercises, strength training, and customized routines to address specific joint concerns while fostering overall body resilience.

Recognizing the diverse range of joint issues and individual injury histories among readers, Hogan underscores the importance of personalized workouts that cater to individual needs. The BFB Training

Program maximizes its effectiveness by incorporating evidence-based techniques and leveraging scientific research. The author advocates for a holistic approach, encouraging readers to view their body's rehabilitation as a nuanced process encompassing both physical and emotional components.

The chapter systematically dissects the BFB Training Program, elucidating various exercises, suitable methods, and the rationale behind their inclusion. Hogan employs principles from rehabilitation and sports science to educate readers about their bodies and the healing process. Additionally, he highlights the significance of consistency and gradual progression in completing the training program, emphasizing the sustained commitment required for enduring results.

Readers gain insights into crafting a personalized exercise regimen aligned with the principles of the BFB Training Program. Hogan's chapter proves beneficial not only for individuals recovering from joint issues but also for anyone seeking to prevent injuries and build a resilient body. In essence, Chapter 12 stands as a pivotal segment in "Built from Broken," offering readers a guide to harnessing the healing potential of targeted exercise and reclaiming command over their physical well-being.

Key Points

1. Prioritize tailored exercise programs that specifically address individual joint needs to facilitate optimal healing and recovery.

2. Embrace a holistic approach to rehabilitation that encompasses both physical and mental well-being, recognizing the interconnectedness of mind and body in the healing process.

3. Commit to consistent and gradual progression in your exercise regimen, adhering to the principles of overload and adaptation to achieve long-term physical improvement and joint health restoration.

Self-Reflection Questions

1. Have you evaluated your current exercise routine and made necessary

adjustments to ensure it aligns with
your specific joint conditions and
recovery goals?

_____

_____

_____

_____

_____

_____

_____

_____

2. Are you incorporating mental wellness practices, such as mindfulness or relaxation techniques, into your rehabilitation plan to promote stress reduction and overall well-being?

_____

_____

_____

_____

_____

_____

3. Are you consistently challenging your body with progressive exercise modifications, gradually increasing the intensity, duration, or complexity of your workouts to stimulate adaptation and improve joint function over time?

_____

_____

_____

_____

_____

_____

Goals

1. Design a personalized exercise plan focused on strengthening and restoring joint health.
2. Implement a comprehensive rehabilitation approach that addresses

both physical and mental aspects of healing.

3. Cultivate a commitment to consistent and gradual progression in your exercise routine, emphasizing long-term sustainability and optimal outcomes.

Action Plan

1. Consult with a healthcare professional or physical therapist to develop a tailored exercise program that specifically targets your joint needs and recovery goals.

2. Integrate mindfulness techniques, such as meditation or deep breathing exercises, into your daily routine to promote mental relaxation and stress

reduction, which can positively impact the healing process.

3. Create a realistic and progressive exercise schedule that gradually increases the intensity, duration, or complexity of your workouts to challenge your body and stimulate adaptation for long-term joint health improvement.

Self-Evaluation Questions for Final Assessment of the Workbook:

1. Did you consistently achieve the goals and objectives outlined in the workbook?

- Yes, I consistently applied the knowledge and skills I acquired from the workbook to complete all assignments and meet all objectives.

2. Did you effectively apply the knowledge and skills learned from the workbook in practical situations?

- Yes, I was able to successfully apply the principles and techniques I learned from the workbook to real-world scenarios, demonstrating my ability to translate theory into practice.

3. How effectively did you manage your time and maintain organization while progressing through the workbook?

- I effectively managed my time and maintained organization throughout the workbook, completing all tasks and assignments within the specified deadlines. I developed a structured approach to my studies, ensuring that I dedicated sufficient time to each module and task.

4. Did you actively seek clarification and support when encountering challenging concepts or tasks in the workbook?

- Yes, I proactively sought clarification and support when faced with difficult concepts or tasks in the workbook. I utilized available resources, such as online forums, discussion groups, and instructor support, to gain a deeper understanding of complex material.

5. Were you able to identify both your strengths and areas for improvement during the workbook completion?

- Yes, I was able to identify both my strengths and areas for improvement throughout the workbook. This reflective process allowed me to focus on my strengths and develop strategies to address my weaknesses.

6. How well did you reflect on your progress and adapt your approach when necessary throughout the workbook?

- I regularly reflected on my progress and adapted my approach as needed throughout the workbook. This self-evaluation process allowed me to identify areas where I could improve my study strategies and enhance my understanding of the material.

7. To what extent did you engage in self-reflection and critical thinking to enhance your understanding of the workbook content?

- I actively engaged in self-reflection and critical thinking to deepen my understanding of the workbook content. I questioned assumptions, analyzed concepts, and considered alternative perspectives to gain a broader understanding of the material.

8. If applicable, how effectively did you collaborate and communicate with others during the workbook activities?

- I effectively collaborated and communicated with others during the workbook activities. I actively participated in group discussions, shared ideas constructively, and provided feedback to my peers.

9. Did you consistently maintain a positive attitude and demonstrate perseverance when facing difficult sections of the workbook?

- Yes, I maintained a positive attitude and persevered through challenging sections of the workbook. I approached difficult tasks with a growth mindset, viewing them as opportunities to learn and develop my skills.

10. How successful were you in integrating the new knowledge and skills from the workbook with your existing expertise?

- I successfully integrated the new knowledge and skills from the workbook with my existing expertise. I was able to apply the concepts and techniques I learned to my current work and personal projects, enhancing my overall competency.

11. Were you able to establish specific goals and monitor your progress effectively as you worked through the workbook?

- Yes, I established specific goals and monitored my progress effectively throughout the workbook. I set clear objectives for each module and tracked my achievements, allowing me to identify areas for improvement and celebrate my accomplishments.

12. How well did you evaluate your own work and provide constructive feedback to yourself during the workbook process?

- I critically evaluated my own work and provided constructive feedback to myself throughout the workbook process.This self-assessment allowed me to identify areas where my work could be improved and make necessary adjustments to enhance its quality.

13. Did you actively pursue additional learning opportunities and personal growth beyond the materials provided in the workbook?

- Yes, I actively sought out additional learning opportunities and personal growth beyond the materials provided in the workbook. I explored online resources, attended workshops, and engaged in discussions with experts to further my knowledge and skills.

14. Were you able to transfer the knowledge and skills gained from the

workbook to other aspects of your life or professional endeavors?

- Yes, I was able to successfully transfer the knowledge and skills gained from the workbook to other aspects of my life and professional endeavors. I applied the principles and techniques I learned to real-world situations, enhancing my problem-solving abilities and decision-making processes.

15. How effectively did you demonstrate creativity, critical thinking, and problem-solving abilities in the workbook exercises?

- I effectively demonstrated creativity, critical thinking, and problem-solving abilities in the workbook exercises. I approached tasks with an open mind, analyzed complex information, and developed innovative solutions to challenges.

_____

_____

_____

_____

_____

_____

_____

_____

Printed in Great Britain
by Amazon

36184947R00071